DREAM

CATCHER

By
Bruce Jones

Copyright © 2007 Bruce Jones
All rights reserved. No part of this book may be used, reproduced or transmitted in any form or manner by any means whatsoever, without the written permission of the publisher except in the case of brief quotations embodied in critical articles and reviews.

Published by Bruce Jones

Cover Design by: Bruce Jones

Photography by: Holly Canuto & Bruce Jones

The author and publisher are not responsible either directly or indirectly for any damages, errors, accidents, or losses either personal or financial to the reader on the part of this work. No warranty or guaranteed results are made.

For more inquiries please email canutojones@gmail.com

Printed in the United States of America

ISBN: 978-0-6151-4861-8

You've found this book for a reason.

Now, You Are Ready.

Take the First Step.

You did not find this book by Coincidence.

But, You will Only Get Out
What YOU Put In.

If you Desire it, You Will Get It.

Every Morning, attempt to recall your dreams. Usually you will have **3 Dreams** in a given night. Each differ in the type of symbols used, but **similar patterns** of symbols used will remain the same. Based on **common features** in each dream and your own **life circumstances** you can **decode** what your dreams are telling you. As you **Record by Writing and Drawing** in this book you will come across additional instructions and things to consider. If you are not successful at first, that is normal. Put your mind to the task and **Results Will Come, be Patient.**

Now, I will leave you to catch your dreams and live from the power of **DREAM WISDOM.**

Sweet Dreams,

Bruce Jones

For my Loving Wife

May your Dreams come True.

LIVE

The

DREAM

DREAMS Learn to live by the messages of dreams. Each of us possesses a deeply spiritual mind whose aim is to help and guide us through life. Your mind processes your past experiences and your higher self gives you feedback on what to do. These messages can range from minor details, ignored in our busy day, to great challenges which have been arranged to obtain a solution.

Morning Record 1

Record 2 "Good Morning"

HIGHER SELF

Yes, You have a Higher Self - your inner true nature. Its goal is to express itself as a way of living from a higher perspective which sees clearly the greater truth. While immersed in worldly trappings and ideas, it's important to distinguish true from false. Recognize that pursuits of the lower mind are immaterial. These pursuits consume thereby overcoming our consciousness making life a nightmare. They haunt us manifesting in our dreams affecting the quality of our life – not just our sleep.

Dream 3 It's good to see you again

Dream 4

MESSAGES There are also the messages of the Higher Self. A pure spirit reaching out to us wanting to make its presence known; waiting for you to bask in its warmth of peace, knowledge and love. It will whisper the great truths of your life. You already have what you need to listen well. Everyone can unlock the powers of their dreams. Spiritual adepts access a wealth of higher knowledge through approaching the dream state. It is our inner selves speaking to us.

Dream 5 Good Morning Sunshine

Dream 6 Keep it up!

ONENESS

There is a oneness to all things, even between the Great Creator and You. You are Connected to and Originate form the One. It is your Birthright to inherit what is yours. It is Given freely and with Love. But the wisdom to use it is for you to discover. It wants to become One with you so that when all false things fade from this world you are closely Connected to the One and You Will Never Let Each Other Go.

Dream 7 The 1st Week of Dreams

A New Week - Dream 1

Record 2 "Good Morning"

LISTEN Listen to the messages which come from the dream state. When your mind is calm and at peace you can focus on the realities that the dream state illuminates to you. You are not perturbed by outside things which are out of tune with your Higher Self. There is only Calm.

Dream 3 It's good to see you again

Dream 4

TRUTH

You have a Higher Self
You are connected to All things
All Things Connect to the One
You come from the One
The One is waiting
Seek the Truth

You are from the Divine Creator and thus you are inherently Divine. Divine is Godly. Godliness is your birthright.

Claim it! **Listen, Learn,** and **Love**.

Commune with the One through your **DREAMS**.

Dream 5 Good Morning Sunshine

Dream 6 Keep it up!

Dream 7 The 2nd Week

LIVE THE DREAM

Have Courage to Follow Your Dreams.
Take a Leap of Faith,
Fear Nothing
Run With It.
Be Bold

Remember the importance of listening to the messages of your DREAMS.

See what is True. See Who You Are.
Live Life with the Fullest of your Human Dignity
— *All is Love*.

www.ingramcontent.com/pod-product-compliance
Lightning Source LLC
Chambersburg PA
CBHW042010150426
43195CB00002B/81